Their F

by Ellen Dalton
illustrated by Nathan Jarvis

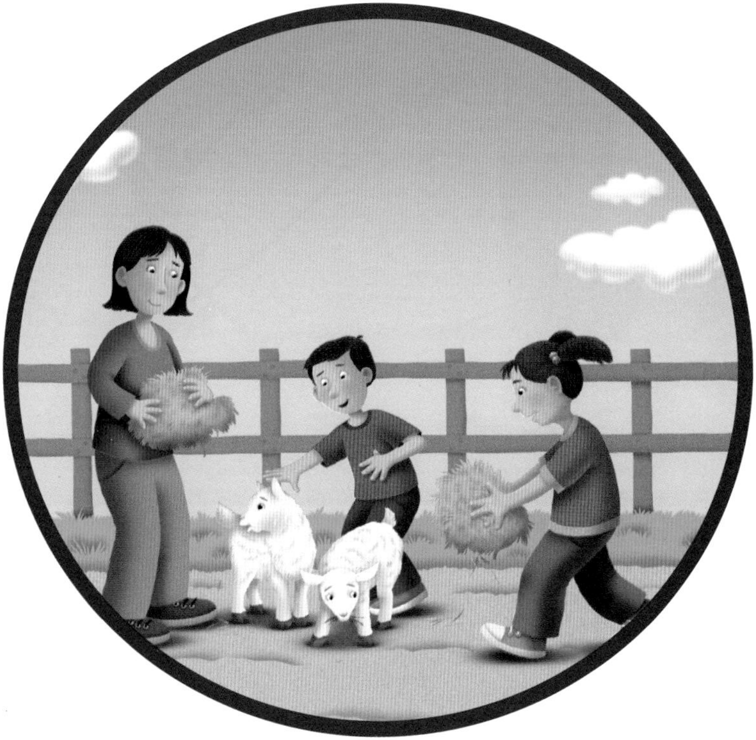

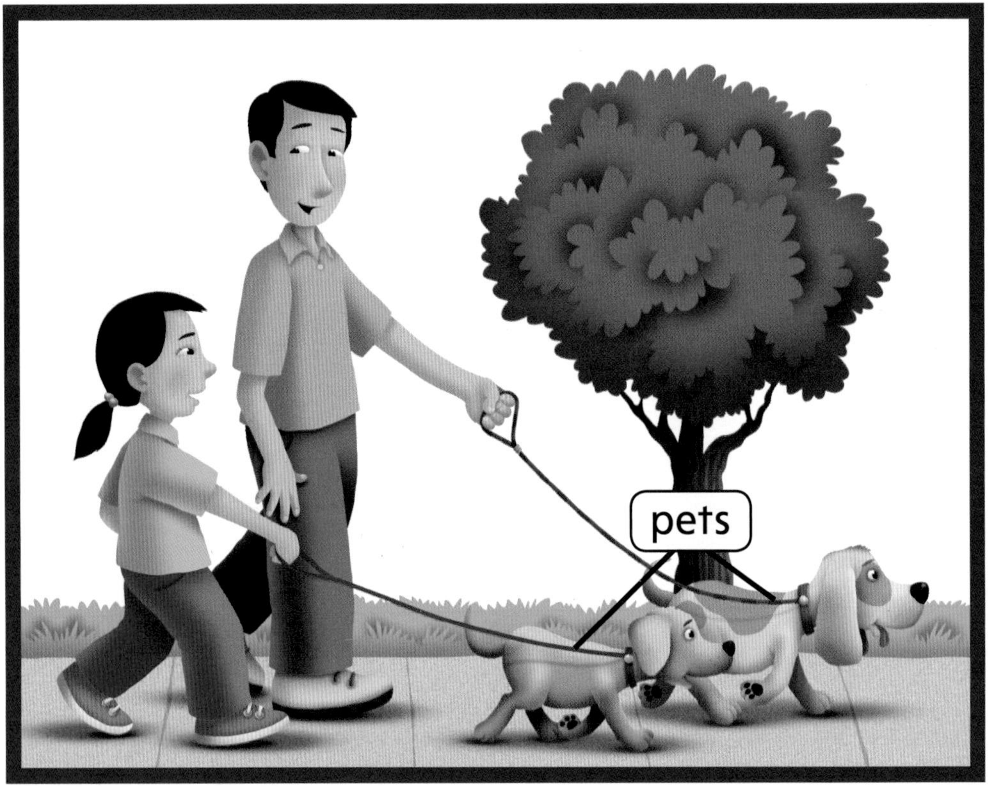

They get walks.

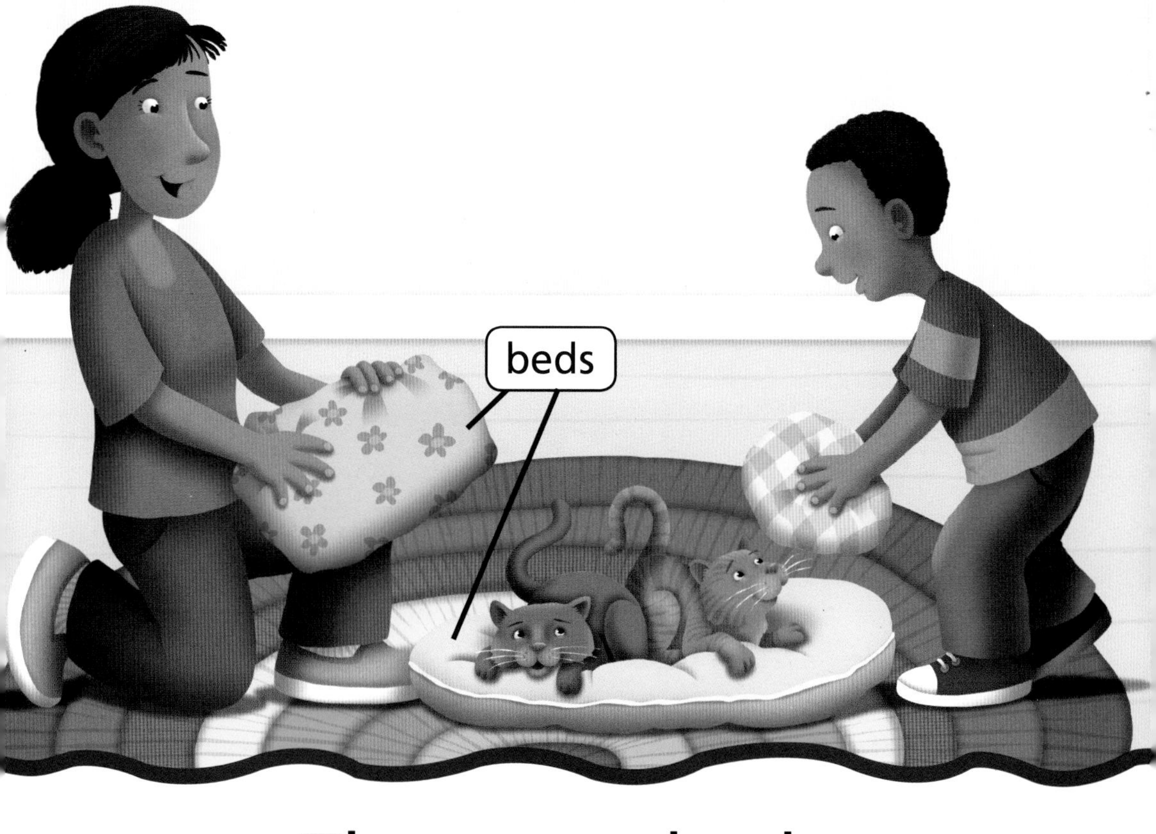

They get beds.

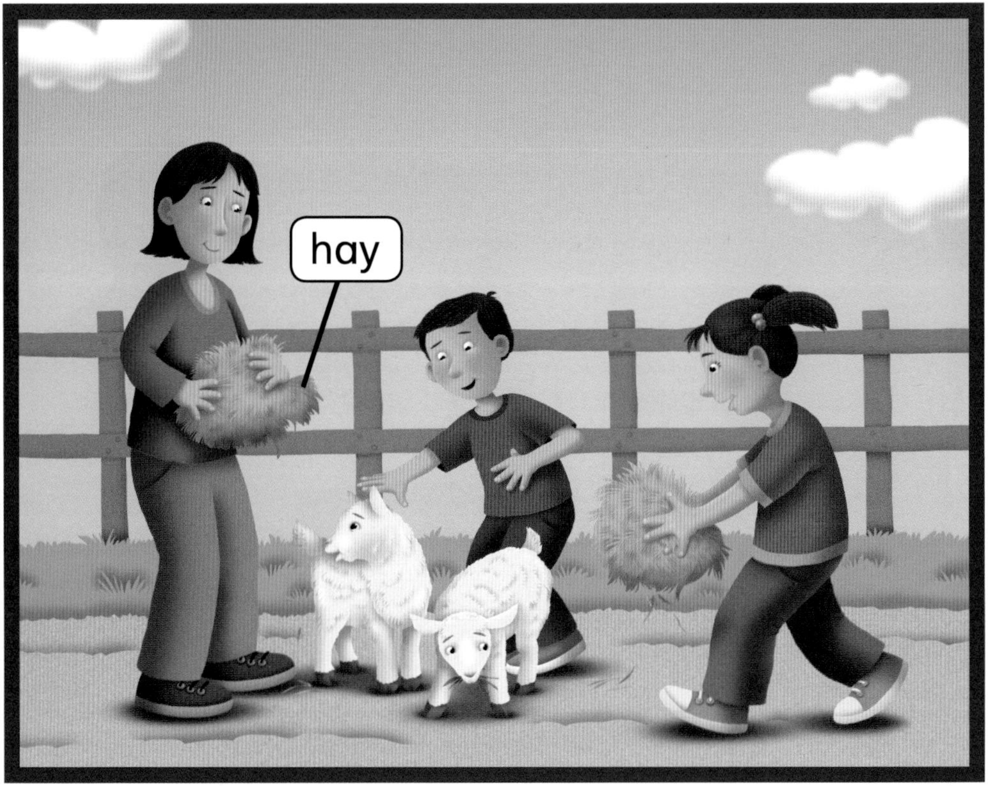

They get hay.

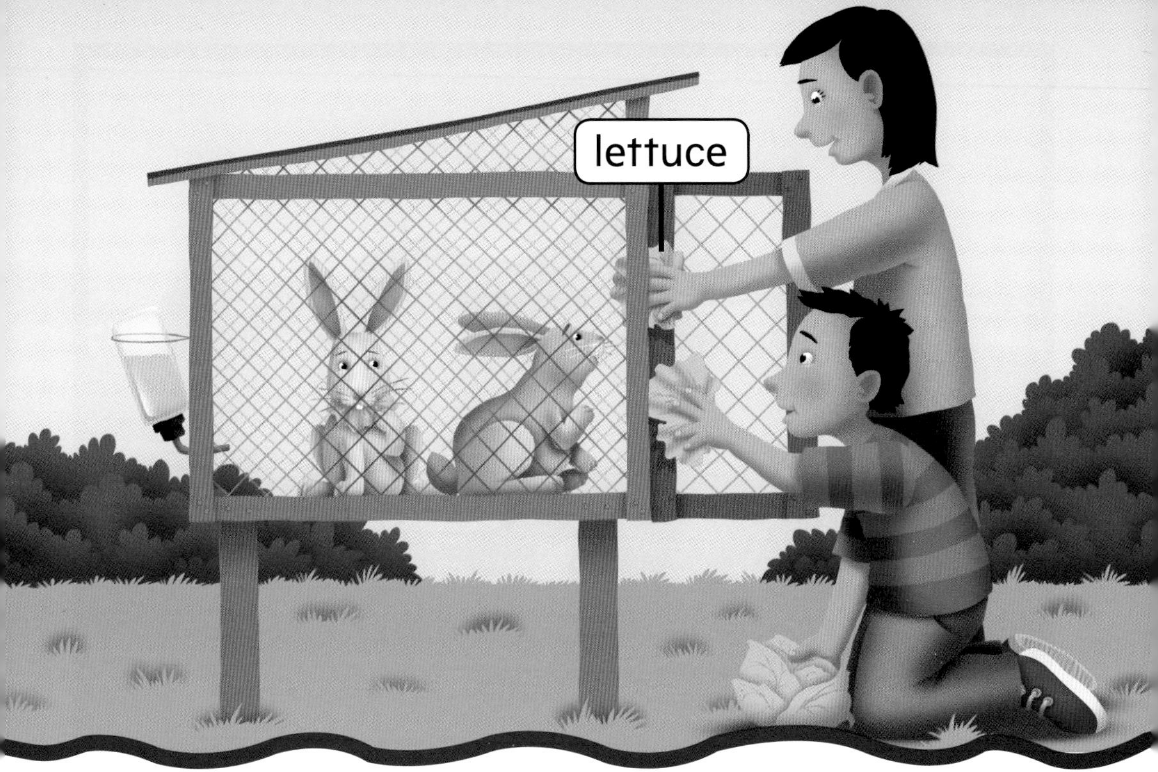

They get lettuce.

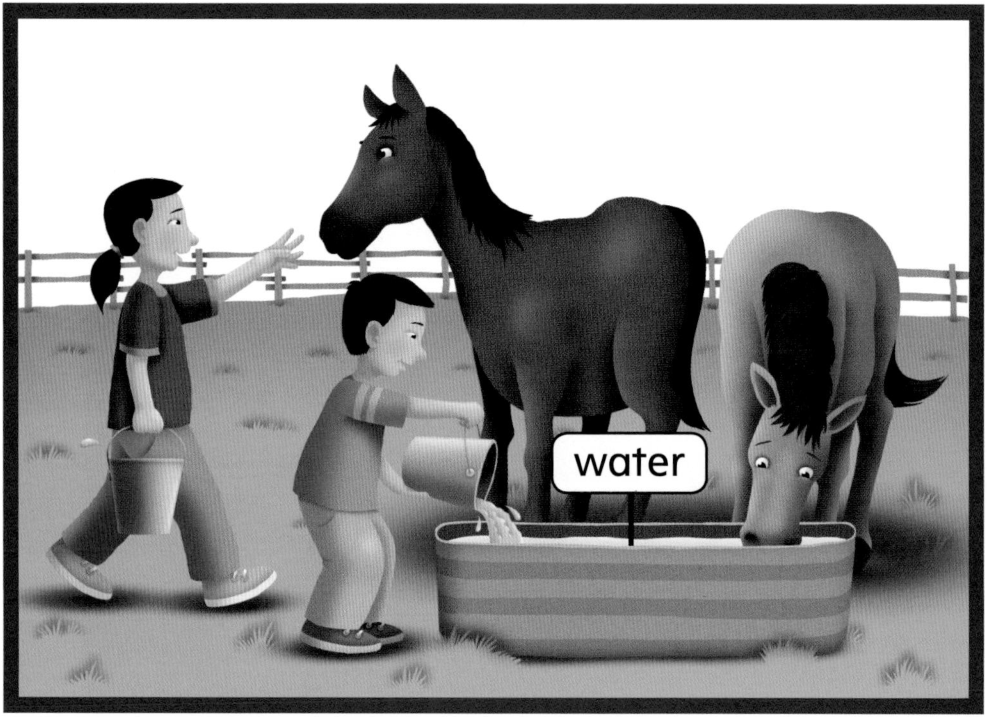

They get water.

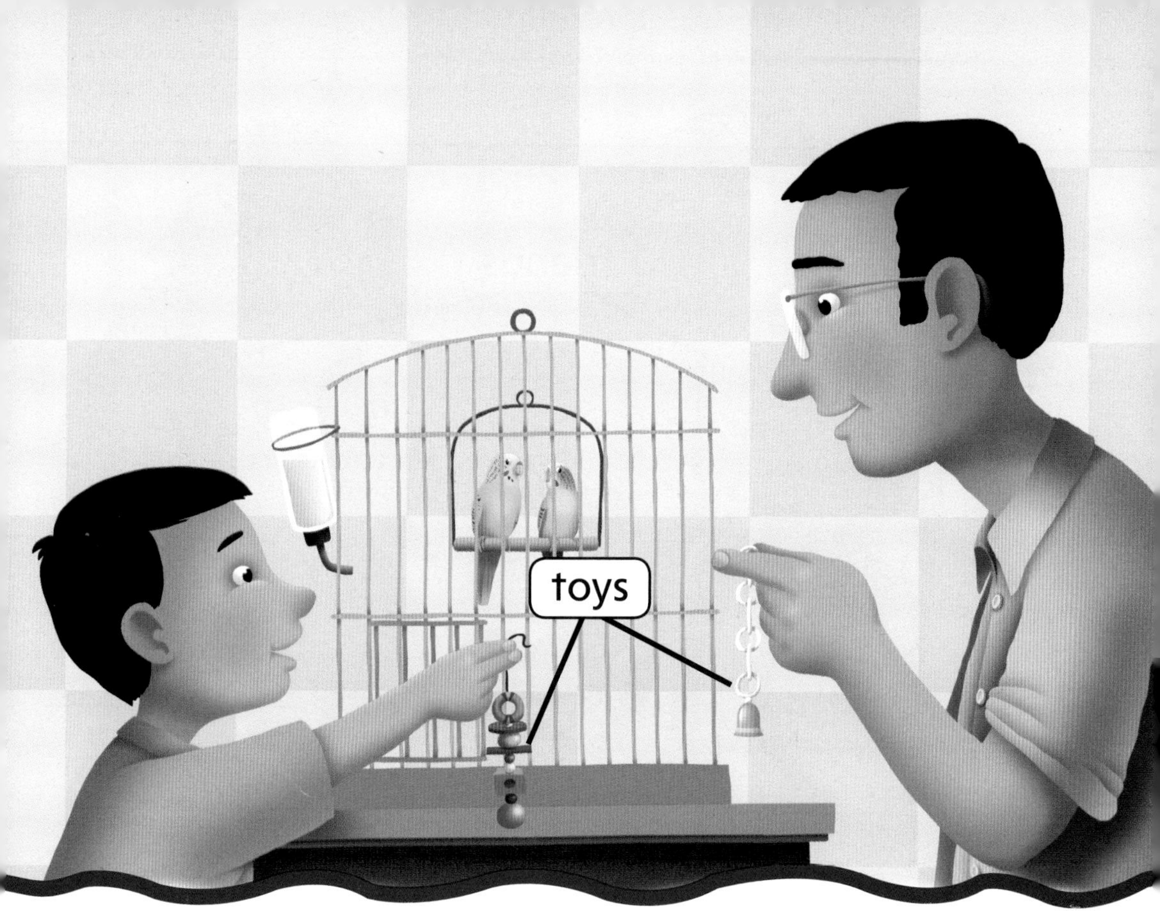

They get toys.

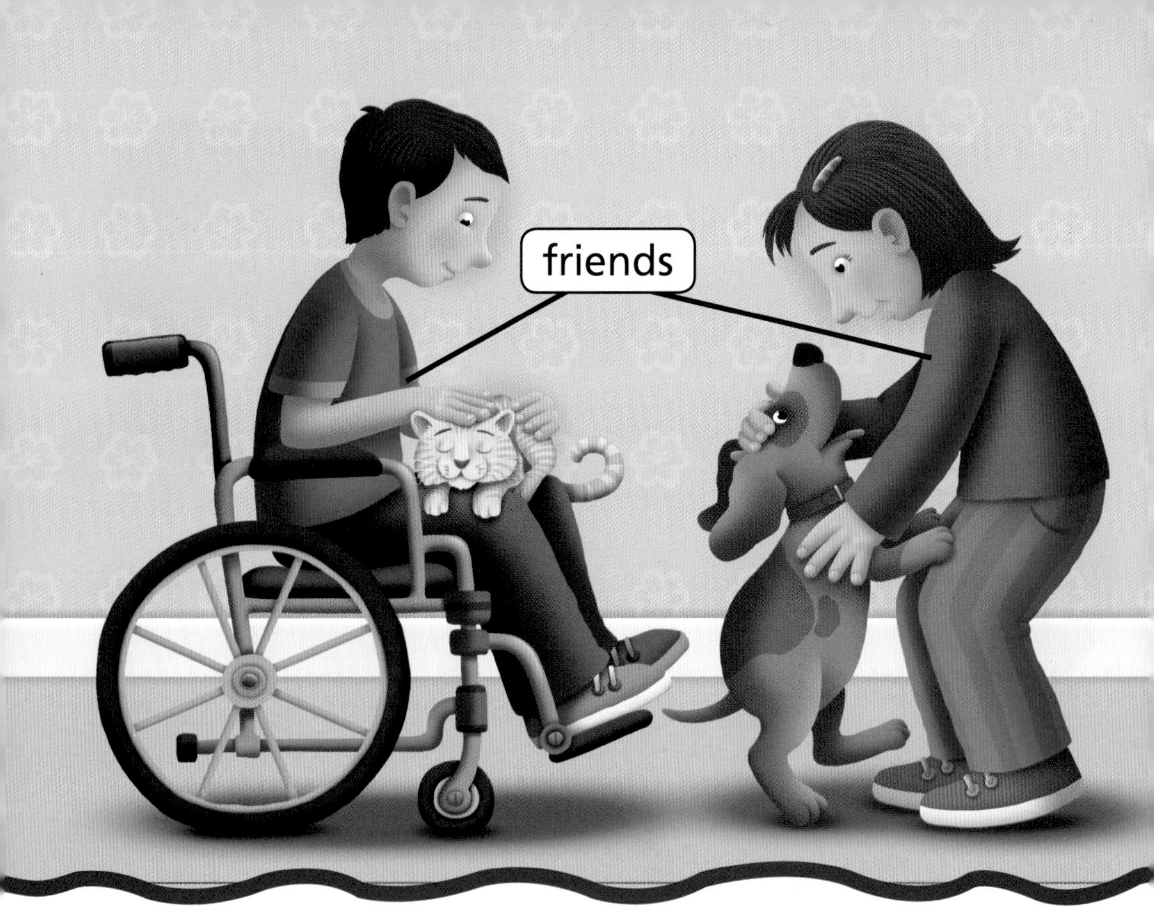

They get friends!